ŞİRİNCE

ONCE UPON A TIME ÇİRKİNCE

Şükrü Tül

EGE YAYINLARI

Series: "Ancient Anatolian Cities"

ŞİRİNCE

Once Upon a Time Çirkince

Şükrü Tül

© 2008 Ege Publications - Şükrü Tül
ISBN 978-975-807-217-0

Cover photograph
Şükrü Tül

Translation
İnci Türkoğlu

Printed at
Graphis Printing House

Production and Distribution
Zero Prodüksiyon
Kitap-Yayın-Dağıtım San. Ltd. Şti.
Abdullah Sokak, No: 17, Taksim
34433 İstanbul
Tel: +90 (212) 244 7521 - 249 0520   Fax: +90 (212) 244 3209
e.mail: info@zerobooksonline.com
www.egeyayinlari.com   www.zerobooksonline.com/eng

CONTENTS

FOREWORD

With the book in your hands, you must first fulfil the requisitions of being a traveller.

I recommend that you start at the Selçuk train station, or at the courtyard wall of the former primary school at Şirince.

You must try to look at the events from these two places within the frame of the events as told in this book.

You must question what the former people of Şirince and the ones today living under the blooming trees with fruits and inside the beautiful houses have suffered.

You must spend some effort abiding by the rules of being a traveller.

As you have this book in your hands and it contains the clues for both stories as many as possible then the rest depends on you.

To me, two pieces of information are lacking: one is the present whereabouts of the former people of Şirince and the second is the life experienced at Kavala and Drama years ago...

I wish that the travellers experience both immigration stories deep inside their hearts.

Şükrü Tül
Archaeologist
November 1995 – March 1996

More words for the second edition:

Şirince has started to deepen her own fate in the flow of time. An indescribable process somewhere in between crumpling and conservation has been swathing the village more and more. The repair of the church has been aborted by the Quatmann Foundation and the former primary school has been converted to a restaurant instead of a museum for it will bring more income accompanied as well as disagreements regarding "whose restoration is better" (!); all these lead us to despair yet interest in Şirince has been increasing. Rarest gifts the time has presented us with are the photos of the visit by İzmir's Governor Kazım Dirik to Şirince about 1930. These photos, which have come from Karşıyaka, show the Pasha first in Ephesos and then in front of the Şirince primary school together with the villagers. On my trip to Greece in 2002, those with Turkish surnames I met in Nea Ephesos village near Salonica reinforced my connections with Şirince. Some more notes arriving with the travel notes by Arundell made it necessary to revise the book. To repeat what I had said earlier, I am sure a clever and sensitive reader will visit Şirince as he or she should, without crumpling.

Şükrü Tül
July 2008

AT AYASULUK STATION

I strongly recommend that you sit down under the plane trees at Selçuk Train Station and watch the railroad and the trains getting more infrequent now. He ruins of ancient Ephesus and Şirince must be taken into consideration together with the opportunities arisen from the trains passing through or stopping here as well as the events occurring around the railroad.

Ephesus has always attracted the travellers for it had the famous Artemis Temple, one of the seven wonders. The ruins of the city extending to Arvalya in the west, Mount Bülbül (ancient Pion or Prion), Mount Panayır (ancient Koressos), slope toward Çamlık, Belevi and the ruins on Ayasuluk Hill have hosted numerous travellers and curious people.

The most curious Turk, who was also a writer, Evliya Çelebi visited Ephesus in 1671 and the ruins were still very dizzying. Evliya Çelebi

Ayasuluk aqueducts, albumin print by Rubellin, about 1880.

Artemision excavations, about 1880, photo: Rubellin.

writes that a visitor would get lost amidst these ruins. Mentioning the air loaded with malaria, Çelebi tells about a square with plane trees, a well with cold water even in the middle of July and houses with earth roofs. On the other hand, with his style of exaggeration Çelebi states that even camels were concealed amidst the lush hemp fields in the plains. Ephesus was known among the local Turks as Ayasuluk around the citadel and the Hellenistic and Roman ruins as Bodurine.

The first excavations at Ephesus were initiated by J. T. Wood, an English engineer working at Ottoman Aydın Railroad Company. The railroad was built in order to exploit the rich produce and raw materials of the region encompassing Aydın, Meander valley, Tire and Ödemiş areas. Especially when raisins and dry figs started reaching the Izmir port via the railroad, the economic process of the region was completed.

Before the Izmir port gained in importance in the 16th century, the local produce was exported from the Kuşadası / Scala Nova harbour. The commercial route toward Aydın was developed by the camel merchants. Thus, the railroad was opposed by the camel merchants first. However, the railroad not only took the local produce to the Izmir harbour but also facilitated the products of Izmir, Istanbul and the rest of world to reach the region. In addition to the Belgian glassware, porcelains, British wares, pocket watches and gas lamps the commerce across the Aegean included the trade of iron consoles manufactured by founders of Izmir, copper *rakı* distillers and oil jars of Lesbos Island via the railroad.

As for the railroad company, the Ottoman government had called for a tender for railroad construction in the country in the newspapers in 1855. A joint venture company was established in the United Kingdom by J. Bahtun, J. Vanilis, W. Cakun and O. Dickson. The company representative R. Wilkin came to Istanbul and received the authorisation in September 1856.

Wilkin and his partners sold their authorisation in May 1857. The company established by Sir Joseph Paxton, Georges Whytes, Augustus Willliam Rixton and William Jackson was named Ottoman Railroads from Izmir to Aydın Company. The company awarded

Hotel Huck, branch at Ayasuluk train station.

the tasks of railroad construction, station facilities construction and purchase of locomotives to a contractor called T. Jackson. The first 70 km long part of the railroad was completed in November 1861 and Ayasuluk was reached. The rest of the road was completed in June 1866. Now the steam engines, the new invention of the world, were running between Izmir and Aydın. The locals called these bizarre engines emitting black smoke as "black steamers (*karavapur* in Turkish)".

Some time later, engineer Wood came to terms with the British Museum and procured the excavation finances. Acquiring the permission of the Ottoman Palace, Wood started excavations in May 1863. His efforts to localise the Artemis Temple did not yield anything for a long time. After digging at various spots, he obtained a clue: a wall uncovered had an inscription stating that it belonged to the *temenos* wall of the temple. This clue was brought together with other bits of information such as that the temple was located 190 m from the temenos wall in the time of Alexander the Great, range of an arrow in the time of the rebel king Mithradates of Pontus and that it was doubled in the time of Marc Antony of the Romans. He proceeded 400 meters north from this wall uncovered in the fields between Selçuk and the Grotto of Seven Sleepers. In 1869 the efforts culminated in the desired result. The location of the temple was spotted below the water level. Many reliefs, architectural elements and votive offerings from Archaic and Hellenistic Artemisions were uncovered. The news spread around the world quickly and Ayasuluk became a focus of interest. The Illustrated London News sent a journalist to the area and published the new finds. As photographs could not be printed due to lack of technology, the view of excavations were printed as engravings.

The number of travellers stopping at Ayasuluk Station increased. Mr. J. D. Karpouza built the Hotel Ephesus on the slope toward Çamlık in 1873. A chubby man with a silver cane in his hand, Mr. Karpouza

Proprietor of Ephesus Hotel at Ayasuluk, J.D. Karpouzas.

13

Hotel Huck today.

spoke English and French fluently and even starred in postcards. However, not long later, a rival appeared for Karpouza who hosted the travellers to Ephesus.

The grandiose Grand Hotel Huck at Pasaport, Izmir, built a branch at Ayasuluk. In some postcards it is given as Hotel Ayasuluk while in some others it is named as Hotel Huck. It was right behind the train station. Hotel Ephesus was pulled down in 1950s, probably during the construction of the modern highway to Aydın built with the notorious Marshall Aid. Yet, Hotel Huck still stands with its single story. Today serving as the lodgement of the Turkish Railroads Inc. it has survived with all its details. It has re-emerged recently as a touristic value with the name Karpouza opposite the rarefying trains. A third hotel was called Hotel Caystros mentioned by the traveller Gaston Deschamps; however, its location is not known today. Also the Baedecker Almanac of 1914 mentions a restaurant named Artemision.

The Ayasuluk station building is of a second, even third degree station building. A single building also including the ticket office, waiting benches under a lean-to roof and its lodgement. It restrooms are outside just like at all stations. A water tank is located on the south. The few lines are arranged according to the manoeuvres of the trains. The structure has preserved its characteristics to a great extent since 1863 and it is an English style building influenced by Victorian period.

Excavations at Ephesus followed one after the other. Finds were taken to London to be displayed at the British Museum. The railroad facilitated the exports of not only the produce but also the historical assets. In 1895, the Austrians started their excavations. Photographs and postcards of Ephesus were printed. Sabah Joalliere at Istanbul issued an album giving a portfolio of available views from Ephesus while Rubellin at Izmir printed 18x24 cm photographs of Ephesus. Another entrepreneur, Monsieur Dermont who also ran the Austrian post office in Izmir, issued postcards of Rubellin's photos.

A postcard editor named Koyunyan sold postcards of Ephesus in his shop in the Franks Street in Izmir... Postcard producer Zachariou Kouri stepped into the business with his emissions from Tenekeli Passage in Izmir. Mr. Molko had postcards of Ephesus printed. Molko's place was at the Forbes Han on the pier and he noted on the back of the postcards that he also dealt in money exchange...

Ayasuluk Station near Ephesus, then excavations, travellers... The people of Çirkince were certainly under the influence of these developments. They were happy when the railroad was under construction that their land's value would increase.

The first guidebook was published by Weber: *Guide du voyageur à Ephese* in 1891. Now let us turn to Şirince...

NATURE

The Çirkince Pass is a valley stretching eastward from Ayasuluk, or modern Selçuk. It is flanked on both sides, especially on the north side, by limestone slopes. The south side has slopes of dark schist. Both stone types were used in the construction of houses at Şirince. To the north of Şirince, on the slopes facing the Küçük Menderes (ancient Caystros) plains is an artificial Roman stone cave known as Kuşini surrounded with high quality marble. Kuşini is only an hour's walk from Çirkince. Following the carriage road, it is a cave at 350 m above the Pranga Ranch.

The Sütini Cave in the Çirkince Pass is mentioned in the novel by Dido Sotiriou. Dr. Erol Atalay surveyed it archaeologically. Sotiriou calls this cave as Sütlü Panhagia, literally "Our Lady with Milk". Atalay's team visited the cave first in 1982 and noted a rock tomb over the entrance, which was very narrow only allowing access by crawling. Its interior has three sections. Completing their surveys in 1983, Dr. Atalay and his team determined that the cave was 70-80 m long. It is known that this cave was in use since 13th century AD. The faded frescoes at the entrance to the cave belong to Christian saints. People from Çirkince had incised various graffiti on the walls, for example: "Sotirikos, the slave of the God," "Oh Christ, please help!" In the novel, Manoli Axiotis and his Turkish friend Şevket describe the cave as here.

"It was impossible to find the entrance to the cave as it was concealed behind large rocks and bushes. After crawling for about 10 meters, one reached a flat area full of stalagmites like thistles. They glimmered shivering in the light of the beacons. At the end of the cave was a bottomless precipice. Once upon a time ago, Şevket and I had discovered this cave but could not dare go to the end of it…"

The view of the cave in the beginning of the century is not any different from the description made by Dr. Atalay in 1980s. The cave is located in the sheer rocky cliff on the left of the road coming from Selçuk.

Şirince, view from the north (2007)

The aqueducts we see as we continue toward Şirince are part of the waterway supplying to the renowned Church of St. John and were built in the Middle Byzantine period. The first ruins of the system are seen near Belevi, continue along the slopes of all the hills parallel to the carriage road and cross the Çirkince Pass. Then the waterway crosses the Selçuk Station and reaches the cistern by the Church of St. John. This canal is known as Pranga Water and its originating point is not known. Traces of water canal observed on the south and west steps of the Belevi Mausoleum should belong to this system. The importance of this waterway system for the Byzantine settlement at Ayasuluk, and perhaps the Ayasuluk of Aydın Emirate should be noted...

Another waterway originates south of Şirince and reaches Ephesus, indeed Ayasuluk. The researchers call it Şirince Water.

The stream flowing through the Çirkince Pass was known as Klaseas in Antiquity. It should have been an important asset of ancient Ephesus together with the Marnas Stream that supplied it because the Selçuk Plains we see today were indeed part of the Aegean Sea in ancient times. The coastal land was narrow and cultivatable land available for ancient Ephesus was limited. Thence comes the importance of Klaseas Valley.

The mountain flanking the Klaseas on the north side is called Mount Elemen in the Turkish period. Its eastern extension is called Mount Selahattin. The hill standing to the west of Şirince is Beylik Hill from where you can see the sea. It also sees the Selçuk Plains below and it rises 508 m. Although the main road to Şirince is via the Çirkince Pass, there is also a path via Beylik Hill.

The hills surrounding Şirince are mainly covered with pine trees. The rocky areas and those opened later are prevailed by maquis. Along the road are anemons and hollyhocks... Many wild olives grow on the slopes by the planes in the stream beds. Olive groves, fig and pear orchards complete the landscape.

Şirince, view of the mosque and the village square.

ITS NAME / ADMINISTRATION

Before Çirkince became Şirince, it was called Kyrkindje, Kirkindsche, Kirkidje, Kırkıca, Kırkınca as evidenced in the renowned maps of Kiepert. It was sort of "ugly" as its name suggested. Although there is no reliable source for it, the story goes that the village called Çirkince, literally "uglily, ickily, hideous", in order to hide its existence. One main story regarding the ugliness is that a group of freed *Rum*s (Greek speaking natives of Turkey are called *Rum* in Turkish as a corrupt form of "Roman" in Arabic) settled at a place designated. Before coming here when they inquired how beautiful the location was, they received an answer saying that "it is uglily!" Thus this name survived until Governor Kazım Pasha visited the village on his touring of all the villages in the province. Then he did not like the name as such a beautiful place must not be called ugly, and asked that its name be changed to Şirince, literally "lovely, cute, dainty".

When we look at the site names ending with –*ce*, we see that there are many in west Anatolia. Dido Sotiriou mentions in her novel a village called Güzel-ce-köy, literally "beautiful-ish-village" near Şirince. It is the modern tiny village of Kuyumcu known for its black population worth noting. These were black slaves who used to work in cotton cultivation. When they were freed, they suffered much of poverty. Kuyumcu is located on the other bank of Küçük Menderes valley, north of Selçuk.

Unfortunately, the main factors affecting the place names, except for the folk stories, are usually neglected. It is impossible to claim that the name Çirkince originated from ancient Anatolian languages, such as corrupted from Kenkrios, the forest of Artemis. The name Çirkince is pure Turkish...

According to Vital Cuinet, in 1890, Çirkince was within the borough of Kuşadası in Izmir *Sanjak* of Aydın Province. For events requiring jurisdiction, one had to appeal to the courts in Kuşadası. In the elections for the Ottoman Assembly of Representatives held in 1912, 16 delegates of Kuşadası voted for İttihat ve Terakki (Union and Progress) Party, one of the two parties participating. 11 of these 16 delegates were Turkish while the remaining 5 were Rums. The opponent party, Hürriyet ve İtilaf (Liberty and Alliance), could not get any votes and the Izmir *Sanjak* had only representative from the Union and Progress Party.

To clarify the population structure of the region, let us have a look at the announcement by Müdafaa-i Hukuk-ı Osmaniye Cemiyeti (Association for the Defence of Ottoman Jurisprudence) on March 17th, 1919... Kuşadası had 20,414 people including 11,100 Muslims, 9,000 Rums, 79 Armenians and 145 Jews. Of course this population includes all those living in an area encompassing Güzelçamlı to Çirkince including Kirazlıyayla. Güzelçamlı, Kuşadası and, above all, Çirkince had a prevalent Rum population. It is possible that Çirkince had the majority of the 9,000 Rums. According to a study by Anasnostopoulos published in Greece, the borough of Kuşadası had 6,189 Rums in total: town of Kuşadası had 2,751, Gavurçamlı (modern

A priest from Şirince and Carl Humann (?) on the right together with the family of E. Purser at Aziziye (modern Çamlık).

Güzelçamlı) 656 Rums. Ayasuluk is noted with 11 Turks and 2782 Rums but how many lived in Çirkince is obscure.

Ayasuluk developed with the Republic and became the centre of a borough with the name Akıncılar; thus, Çirkince became a village of Akıncılar in the province of Izmir. Then in 1927, Selçuk became the centre and encompassed Kuşadası as well. In 1957, Kuşadası was taken in Aydın Province while Selçuk became the centre of a borough in Izmir Province.

The churches of Çirkince were subject to the bishopric in Aydın. The see of this bishopric called Heliopolis ("the city of the sun") covered a large area extending from Torbalı to Birgi, to Denizli and entire southwest Turkey down to Fethiye. Heliopolis together with other bishoprics in west Anatolia such as Ephesus, Izmir, Philadelphia (modern Alaşehir) was under the authority of the Greek Orthodox Patriarchate at Fener, Istanbul... The inscription above the gate of Hagios Yannis (St John the Baptist) Church in Çirkince states that it was under the authority of Heliopolis bishopric.

As we learn from the novel by Dido Sotiriou, the Ottoman administration was represented in Çirkince by the gendarmerie sentry.

EARLIEST TRACES / SHORT HISTORY

The earliest structure known in Şirince dates back to the Hellenistic period, possibly from the time of Lysimachus when Ephesus was re-founded. It has been exposed during cleaning work in the recent years and it is known as a monastery among the locals; however, it is disputable whether or not it actually was a monastery. The ruins indicate that the original structure was altered; shortly, this is a tower. A rectangular structure, its east wall has survived in good condition while its north wall is buried and the west wall has survived as a few courses of stones. The most important of all is the fine, stone south wall facing the stream below. This south wall is 9.48 m wide and it is

Remains of a monastery to the north of Şirince.

7.90 m deep in the part where it sits on the slope. The south wall comprises only two courses of stones rising 32 cm in height. The structure is divided in two with a wall of the same stones. The wall and plaster coating the stone courses on the south indicate that the structure has an internal partitioning. This alteration was done in the Byzantine period. Making use of the inner partitioning during the last phase of use, a small chapel was built here occupying one half of the Hellenistic tower and extending as a long room accessed from the west. By the apse are rectangular niches on the left side. Just to the left and right of the doorway is a window on the long sides. Today the structure looks like a simple barn but a research considered it as a "temple-church" for the Hellenistic structure could be a temple. Where is it? Well, past the mill, a few hundred meters above the road climbing up toward Şirince, on the left. On the surface are numerous potshards and one piece belonged to a crater of the 4th century BC. Similar structures are also found around Ephesus.

This tower must have been built in the Klaseas Valley for the early warning system of Ephesus. In Şirince, the most visible Byzantine ruin is the jars displayed in front of the coffee houses. One such jar is in front of the pension no. 156 in İstihlas quarter. These gigantic size jars have a form that suggest Byzantine make. Used for storing oil or wine, these jars must have survived from the cellar of a house.

A bread stamp found in the peach orchard of Ali Kaya must be the most important find from the Byzantine period. The baked clay stamp bears the name Georgios and has a cruciform decoration. It indicates the presence of life here in the Byzantine period because a producer willing to sell honest bread with a brand suggests the presence of a community at Çirkince, although very small.

Despite the lack of evidence for the foundation of Çirkince, the story goes that when Ephesus disintegrated, the harbour shifted to Kuşadası (or Scala Nova as the Franks called it) and a small group moved up the mountains. Another small population remained around the tomb of St. John. When the Byzantine Emperor Justinian built a monumental church over the tomb in the 6th century, the importance of historical and religious events that had taken place here must have kept a small population sticking to living here.

The monastic remains around are said to be here since the 9th and 13th centuries. The best-known and easiest to reach is located to the north of the village. Known as Manastır, i.e. monastery, this area is also rich in emery. The courtyard borders of this monastery can be discerned with bushes and piles of stones. The courtyard extends longer than 150 meters in the east-west direction and the building in its centre has a curious architecture for the entrance. An arched fore-room enhances the outlook of the building. The oblong room behind is obviously the basement as inferred from the ventilation pipes in the walls. Its east wall has niches. The remains of niches on the upper floor forming the ground

The Byzantine jar at the house no. 156 in İstihlas Quarter of Şirince.

level suggest a curious layout. The building possibly had a second floor and potshards around suggest the 13ᵗʰ century as a date.

During the period when Turks settled in the region and especially at Ayasuluk some records indicate the presence of Çirkince in the 16ᵗʰ century. The pious foundations book of Aydın no. 571 and dated to 1583 in the archives of Ankara Title Deeds and Cadastre General Directorate mentions the name of Çirkince. This book contains the list of land owned by pious foundations within the borders of Çirkince sub-district. The lands at Ezine, Kızılca, Ulucak and Turgud were endowed by the "late İsa Bey" according to the registers. All these villages were called as "villages subject to Çirkince"… This İsa Bey must be the son of Mehmet Bey, son of Aydın. Turks developed Ayasuluk and environs mostly in the reign of İsa Bey. İsa Bey Mosque was constructed in 1375. When Cüneyd from the same dynasty was killed in 1425/26, the region passed into the Ottoman hands.

The earliest travel diary mentioning Çirkince is the *Travels in Turkey and back to England by the late Reverend and Learned Edmund Chishull, B.D., Chaplain to the Factory of the Worshipful Turkey Company at Smyrna*. Edmund Chishull visited Turkey between September 12ᵗʰ 1698 and February 10ᵗʰ 1702.

Chishull departs from Tire toward Ephesus ruins on April 30ᵗʰ 1699. As inferred from his narratives, the only place for overnighting near Ephesus was Kirkinceköy, *köy* meaning village in Turkish. When they reached Belevi, they saw the Keçi Kalesi ('Goat Castle') where it was said that dervishes dwelled. The marshy ground at the bottom of the castle was known as Stagnum Pegaseum in Antiquity; it was a lake where Küçük Menderes River joined.

Their guide misguided and took them away from Çirkince. Then they learned the correct route and following the Pass to the east of Ayasuluk Hill, they reached the village.

"… Under his guiding we rode our horses for an hour and a half starting from the Citadel of Ephesus. Exhausting and long, but pleasant and nice route took us between two hills with a stream with waterfalls. On either side of us were myrtles, oleanders, brooms, redbuds, lilacs and other pleasing trees bestowing us with dark shades…"

Chishull's account helps us identify the location of the mill at the bottom of the ramp and where even today the water purls.

Chishull should have considered the purling waters before going into the mill as a waterfall.

Chishull and his party reached Çirkince about 8 o'clock and spent the night in the tents put up by the muleteers.

Next morning, on the 1st of May, they strolled in the village thinking that it was built on the Church of Ephesus, which was one of the seven churches of the Book of Revelation. According to the information they give, all the villagers were Christian.

"The priest of the village wanted to show us the so-called hand-written manuscripts of the evangelists. He showed a Gospel which he claimed to have been written by Prochorus, one of the seven men chosen to serve as mentioned in the Acts of the Apostles. Our close examination showed that the letters dated to the 6th, perhaps even 7th century. The book was either a copy of the Bible or a prayer book."

Chishull and his party left Çirkince that day in the afternoon and settled at a *han* in Ephesus.

Another traveller, Reverend F.V.J. Arundell of Smyrna visited Çirkince in 1833 on his way back to Izmir from exploring the Antioch in ancient Pisidia. Arundell tells about the stories on Mehmet the Bald of Atça, the *zeybek* who revolted against the Ottomans. He also notes his memories on Çirkince which he saw in May 1832 first time... They reached the village in a rainy afternoon and spent the night. Next morning, they talked with the two priests of the village. The locals were trying to build a school then. Arundell and his friends were taken to the school "room" adjoining the church and they saw that the lowest level of education was given by a teacher who had a single eye only under the worst conditions possible. Then as they wanted to go to a coffee house the single-eyed teacher and a priest tried to show them the documents of proficiency they had obtained from the Turkish authorities. In November 1833, Arundell left his friends Dethier and Kyriakos behind in Ayasuluk and visited Çirkince again for he was interested in this village for some correspondence and religious cooperation.

Bread stamp of "Georgios" from the garden of Ali Kaya.

"The road lay through a narrow ravine or valley, with the deep bed of a river, probably the Kenkrios, all the way on the right, and after some time we saw the small remains of an aqueduct on the left, and not long after a mill on the right. Leaving the valley at a quarter before five, in a quarter of an hour after came to a fountain of fine water, and magnificent plane trees, and enormous rocky mountains.

We ascended by a succession of staircases of rocks, hearing the rush of the river on the left at an immense depth below. ...The village is a considerable one, of at least three hundred houses, all Greek:the principal language of the villagers is Turkish, though they know something of their own tongue."

As soon as Arundell reached the village, he went out to find the single-eyed teacher he had known from the year before. As he expected, he found the two priests and the teacher at the door of the school. Wit the requests by Georgios, his friend, he went to talk to the village council of elders in order to find a priest for the village. And he was also shown the famous manuscript, just as was Chishull. According to Arundell this was a dictionary and beginnings of various chapters were illuminated. As its cover was removed the priests told him to kiss it and also claimed that this book was written down personally by St. John the Theologian. However, the first page indicated that it was brought from Crete or Samos and its last repair and binding were done in 1787. Arundell talked to the village headman at the church and told him his wishes for the school.

"We now went to the hospitable mansion of my friend Georgios. The whole family knew me from window, and gave me the warmest welcome. The old mother was, as usual, seated on the ground with her wheel, and with twenty Turkish words, and one Greek, asked me a thousand questions, and gave me a thousand welcomes. Georgios' wife was occupied with her child at the breast, but was warm in her attentions as the old woman; so were several other women, and all, but one of children, who run away and hid himself in affright, seemed rejoiced to see me once more.

Leaving some modern Greek testaments for the use of church, and some small books for the use of ten boys at the school, we quitted Kirkinge, but in doing so, took a road which a wrong one. We were kindly directed to the right one by numerous villagers whom we met returning from their work in the plain below. Most of these were females, and dressed in the Turkish manner, covering their faces with all the real unaffected feeling of native innocence.

In fact, this little population of probably fifteen hundred persons, interested me more than any Greeks I have ever met with. The men

The primary school built with "sarımsak" stone in 1900s.

Marble fountain in the yard of the former primary school.

are all armed as the Turks, with pistols and yatagan, a privilage which they have well merited, from having often successfully used them against the Samiote robbers; many of whom have been killed by the men df Kirkinge."

"It is time so return to my friends Dethier and Kyriacos. We remounted our horses at half past one, and on leaving Aiasaluk and winding round the castle, ..."

Later Arundell learned that the grocer Georgios of Çirkince went on pilgrimage and continued his efforts for the school...

Looking at the events when Arundell travelled we see a period when autonomous Greek (*Rum*) settlements such as Ayvalık prospered and shone. In this phase when the central authority weakened gradually, agricultural produce and commercial organisations developed increasingly and supplemented the power of the land owners. Land owners like the *ayan*s in west Anatolia were semi-autonomous, collected taxes, reported to Istanbul, had armed men; above all, they took the place of appointed officials. In this process, some Rum settlements prospered with the coming of the Rums from the islands who agreed to become tax-payers. The settlements became cities on the condition that they paid their taxes and stayed under the gendarmerie control. Ayvalık is the largest example; Alaçatı is a medium size one while Çirkince is smaller and Domatia near Söke being the smallest.

When Greece won her independence in 1821 the Rum population came under pressure but a systematic increase in population was supported by the Hellenic governments. In the province of Aydın the Rum population increased until 1880s. This was due to the demand on artisans and development of agricultural areas based on the demand by the merchants.

The period continued in peace and with little problems until the First World War. With the loss of territory in the Balkans the local minorities were once again put under pressure. The Battalions of Workmen mentioned in the novel by Sotiriou emerged thus.

Defeat at the First World War provoked the regional desire for independence.

"The Germans left all the arsenals back in ancient Ephesus. With the order of Mondros Armistice these arsenals were to be handed over to the Allied Forces but the Turkish gendarmerie to do so fled. And the locals of Kırkıca village strode the ways to ancient Ephesus in the dark and carried all the weapons and ammunitions to the village. Then, they felt themselves free. The humpy backs straightened. Even the most coward ones carried cartridge belts and walked proudly, like toughies, as if saying to Turks "Dare to come now!""

All these were followed by the Greek invasion of Izmir on the 15th of May 1919. Ayasuluk was occupied on the 22nd of May. The region stayed under Greek occupation until September 1922. Then passing into Turkish hands, this time the problem of population exchange started.

All these stages are also found in the novel by Dido Sotiriou. Thereafter, the problems of the refugees coming from Kavala and Thessaloniki are told in the story Çirkince in Sırça Köşk ('Crystal Mansion') by Sabahattin Ali.

SETTLEMENT

The settlement is said to have had 1800 houses; however, today about 200 houses have survived. Thus, Arundell's account for 300 houses in 1833 is plausible. Settlement is observed dense starting on the hill with the primary school on the slopes rising toward south and facing north; however, proceeding eastward and looking toward the hills on the south, you will also see houses. On the ridge forming the west of the Upper Church is a gigantic plane tree but the fountain underneath it has disappeared. On the slope descending northward from the plane tree was a row of shops as claimed by the locals but there is no clear evidence for this. A tiny stream bed descending toward the modern mosque from the ridge with the Upper Church and stretching between the houses facing east and those facing north and this bed divides the settlement into two. The quarter to the east of this stream bed is called İstiklal meaning 'independence' while the quarter on the west of it is called İstihlas meaning 'rescue'. İstihlas

View of the İstihlas Quarter from the west.

quarter reaches down to the flat grounds starting below the slopes facing north and here a street cutting it and forming the market area.

The street terminates in the shade of a large plane tree and it is flanked with coffee houses, bakeries and shops. An oil press is at the easternmost point while a second one is at the northernmost point. In the northernmost part, on a lower hill at the end of the ridge with the houses is the primary school building.

This primary school is the most important stop to get to know the topography of Şirince. You can easily see and watch the overall view of the houses, orchards and the mountains in the north. Above the stream that borders the settlement in the east was a laundry once upon a time ago. It was still in use during the Republic era but then disappeared. Further east is the cemetery.

Houses, huts in the orchards and vineyards, monasteries and chapels all but disappeared; however, only where those who still remember something point at you can find some traces. One of the most important mills of the village is located at the point where the road starts climbing up the Çirkince Pass and the water still runs there. Remains of walls for the water canals of two more mills are found on the south slopes, opposite the aqueducts at the end of the road at the start of the Çirkince Pass.

PANHAGIA KAPULU

The discovery of the House of the Virgin Mary is connected with the people of Çirkince. Their tradition of commemorating her death on the 15th of August every year proved that the Virgin died in Ephesus.

A nun called Anna Katherina Emmerich described through her visions the place and house where the Virgin lived although she was thousands of kilometres away and bed-ridden.

However, her descriptions did not call any attention. German poet Clemens Brentano was interested in the visions of Emmerich who had never been to Ephesus and visited her in 1818. He wrote these visions down after Emmerich died in 1824 but his dream of publishing them was also delayed when he died in 1842. His brother Christian took

over the duty but could not reach the goal. Following his death in 1851, the book titled *Life of the Blessed Virgin Mary* was finally published in Frankfurt between 1851 and 1855 by his friends in nine divisions.

In the light of Katharina Emmerich's visions and on the order of the principal of the Lazarist College at Izmir, Eugene Poulin, a group including Reverend Henry Jung, Reverend Vervault, Thomaso, their guide Pelekas and a local black Muslim guide from the region joining them started their explorations around Ephesus in 1891. On the 29th of July, the team with the Emmerich's book in their hands learned the presence of a spring nearby from the people of Çirkince working their tobacco fields behind Ephesus. Where they went to was a sacred spring. They could see the sea and Ephesus from that point, just like Emmerich had said. Remains over the spring belonged to an old church...

Poulin visited and investigated the ruins himself on 12th of August. The remains were re-explored and photographed on the 19th and 25th of August. Now they were certain that this was a holy site, house of the Virgin Mary. The headman of the village and lawyer Constantinidis told the story of their traditions on October 14th, 1892 as follows:

"... Following the crucifixion of Christ, our Lord, the Holy Virgin Mary, Mother of God, lived in Ephesus with the entrustment to Apostle John... Then she was taken to Mount Bülbül... there she died (Dormition) at her home at Kapulu and we commemorate this every August..."

Priests who came to explore the house of the Virgin describe Çirkince of 1892 as an orthodox town with a population of 4,000 and mostly speaking Turkish. The Çirkince people retained this information regarding the Virgin after Ephesus became part of history and for example in 1864 they also repaired the walls of Panhagia Kapulu and took on its guarding.

The house of the Virgin Mary is a place of visit by the Christendom and Islamic world today and it should be considered a gift of Çirkince people.

DIDO SOTIRIOU
1909-2004

Dido Sotiriou was born in a Turkish bathhouse in Aydın. Her father was a soap seller. When she visited Turkey, journalist Handan Şenköken from Izmir helped her find that bathhouse. She migrated to Athens together with the family in 1922 and finished university despite her family's objections and started working at the university. She worked in the underground press during the German occupation (1940-45) and joined the resisters.

Her works:

- *I Nekri Perimenoun / The Dead Wait*, 1959, novel
- *Ilektra (Anagenisis) / Elektra – Rebirth*, 1961, novel
- *Matomena Chomata / Bloodied Earth (Farewell Anatolia)*, 1962, novel
- *Mikraasiatiki Katastrophi ke i Strategiki tou Imberialismi Anatoliki Messogio / The Catastrophe of Asia Minor and the East Mediterranean Adventure of Imperialism*, 1975, research
- *Mesa Stis Floges / In Flames*, 1979, novel
- *Katedalphisametai / We were falling*, 1982, novel

The writer was awarded the Abdi İpekçi Prize of Turkish-Greek Friendship in 1982. The novel *The Dead Wait* tells a story starting in Aydın and continuing in Izmir and then in the refugee quarter of Piraeus and it was translated into the Turkish in 1995 and published by Arion Publishers.

TRADITIONS

Perhaps adding her own memories of Aydın, Dido Sotiriou describes Çirkince with the words she had listened from Manoli Axiotis as follows:

"Each villager was the lord of his own piece of land. Everybody had a two-storied house in the village. In addition, a summer home surrounded with walnut, almond, apple, pear and cherry trees and vegetable gardens. And nobody neglected to decorate their gardens with flowers. And the streams springing on all sides never stopped flowing… When the wheat and barley were ripe our fields were like gold gilt seas. You would never find elsewhere olive trees such as ours, full of olives so much that the branches touched the ground, round and black olives, glimmering olive trees. Olive oil was a slow but reliable source of income. But figs… Figs filled the belt of the villagers with gold! Our figs were famous not only in Aydın province but also in the East, Europe and America. Such a thin skin almost non-existing, honeyed with the sun of Anatolia…"

Embroidered wall decoration made by Şirince people at Nea Ephesos by Thessaloniki, Greece.

Fountain at the İstihlas Quarter.

The railroad passing by the village so abundant also provided a chance for consumption. Among the vendors coming to the station were not only merchants bringing goods from Izmir shops but also those who grilled the fish caught in the nearby lakes.

Then, in the summer the village was abandoned. They all moved to their huts in the countryside, to those down in the plains. They came back with the autumn.

A farmer family from Çirkince.

An example of the rare three-story houses.

"… They returned back to the village as the time for Hagios Demetrios festival approached. Women would launch their house paintings and autumn cleanings. It was their custom to cleanse all from the kitchen wares to the street. And the village was so cleansed that you would not want to walk in the streets."

For such a cleansed spot, we can cite the house with a bench in front on the way to the Lower Church from the house of the physician.

Izmir was one of the places to spend money when the produce was sold. Those who went to Izmir always bought new clothes, tried to enjoy the social life at the Promenade, the Kordon... They took the train to go to Izmir. Autumn was also the season for wedding festivals.

In the season of cherries, the Feast of Hagia Triada ('Holy Trinity') was celebrated. The young men fitted their *yataghans* in their belts and strolled around

Fountain with cross int he village square.

with their blue broadcloth costumes. The women strolled on the back of their husbands' horses, wearing the strings of gold on their heads. It was customary to play the dulcimer and *kemençe* (string instrument) in the countryside. Songs played in such entertainment in the countryside were called *Glendjedika*, literally "songs for entertainment".

On the first day of Lent, everybody went to the countryside, roasted chestnuts, drank *rakı* to celebrate this special day. The married ones would tell the stories of their first meeting and their weddings. Single ones were not admitted to such gatherings.

Those who decided to get married had to build a house. When the candidate started to dig for the foundations of the house, the neighbours would give him a hand.

They picked the olives from October through February; removed the wild weeds in February and March; cultivated their tobacco from March to July; then in the autumn, the grapes, raisins and figs took their turns.

NOT WITHOUT IZMIR

An interesting story from the novel is the love story from Güzel-
ceköy, whose localisation is obscure, and where Manoli Axiotis went
to. The love between Artemisa, the worker, and Ali, the lord of the
farm, was a liaison and sets an example for the attitudes that avoided
the connections between the Rums and Muslims. Yet Ali Bey won the
heart of Artemisa but an Izmir song was sung to announce that this
love was no good. The song told about Eli, who eloped with a gendarmerie officer, abandoning her husband; so she was reproached.
According to the beliefs, she was to be killed with a knife with two
sharp edges because it was the God's order not to marry a Turk, not
to love a Turk.

Manoli Axiotis witnessed the story of another song. When the fig
shop in Izmir he was working at sold out, he found himself in the
street. First he worked at a horseshoer, then found another job at the
han of the notorious toughie Louloudias. There he was influenced by
the singers and Louloudias who hated Turks. Ogdondakis (Yannis
Dragatzis), one of the singers, was involved in a bad situation. One
woman, whom he did not indulge, informed against him saying that
he was a spy. Imprisoned, Ogdondakis ate the dinner and drank the
rakı before going to the gallows. Getting anxious, he sang a song.
Süleyman, the pasha of the jail, heard the song and summoned him
to his mansion.

Ogdondakis sang his song "Aman Memo, Şeker Memo" and was
released from death sentence. Adjutant released him off his handcuffs
and told him to go away, so he went to Greece via Samos. But the
song already became popular the next day. This famous song was
recorded in 1928 by the famous singer Kosta Nouro. All Turkish lyr-
ics, the song tells about a hidden and moving love story.

It is included in the novel as a result of the memory of perhaps
Dido Sotiriou or perhaps Manoli Axiotis.

MEMO

Ah! aman aman, şekerim aman, cilvelim aman
[Oh! Help! Sweetie, Cutie, help!]
aman aman / Şu dereden boyun ermiş
[Oh, dear! / Your height has passed over the creek]
Aman Memo, ufak Memo, şeker Memo,
[Oh, dear Memo, little Memo, sugar Memo]
sevdalı Memo gel
[lovesick Memo, come]
Ah! varın bakın neler olmuş/ aman aman
[Oh! Dear, go and see what has happened/ oh, dear, help]
aman, dertli Memo, yanık Memo gel
[oh, dear, suffering Memo, elegiac Memo, come]
aman aman / Alın gelin kırık kalplimi
[oh, dear / please bring here my heart-broken darling]
alın gelin kırık kalbimi
[oh, dear, please bring here my broken heart]
seven..... (anlaşılmıyor)
[loving... (not clear)]
aman Memo, kıymatlı Memo, sevdalı Memo gel
[Oh, dear Memo, precious Memo, lovesick Memo]
ah güzel yüzün (Rumcasını söylüyor)
[oh your beautiful face (then sings in Greek)]
/yarda bile yok Memo Memo
[even the darling does not have it, Memo, Memo]
aman aman kaymak Memo ...Memo,
[Oh, dear, oh help, delicious Memo]
dertli Memo gel
[oh, dear, suffering Memo, come]

HOUSES / MOSTLY TWO-STOREYED

Before telling about the houses of Şirince, we have to mention the development of Turkish house typology. The example uncovered in Pougachenkova in Central Asia is square in shape and has a room in each corner separated from each other by a *sofa* in the middle. The Anatolian house was originally a *megaron* which was arranged for the heat of the summer and cold of the winter. The *megaron* type house is seen since the first layer of Troy. The Hellenes, i.e. ancient Greeks, surrounded the *megaron* with a row of columns on all sides creating the house of the gods.

A house with a shop downstairs, İstihlas Quarter.

Hand-made decoration at a roof corner.

The house with decorated under-eaves, İstiklal Quarter.

House door with dragon, İstiklal Quarter.

Plaster pigeon decorating the corner of the eaves.

Turkish house with a *sofa* is a joint version of both house types and is known as of the 16th century.

This house type has a *sofa* between the rooms, a semi-closed *hayat*; its uncountable variations can be followed as of the 18th century mainly. Very common across Anatolia, this house type is sort of synthesized at Şirince with the Christian faith. The *hayat* cannot be clearly seen as is the case with the houses of Muğla. The *hayat* and courtyard seen in the houses of Muğla are the result of the Muslim faith and introverted way of life. However, the appearance of the houses formed with the same concerns, proportions and functions.

İzmir-type house (on the right), İstiklal Quarter.

Twin houses, İstiklal Quarter.

Wall painting, İstiklal Quarter.

Among the houses, which are mostly two-storeyed, are also single-storeyed and multi-roomed examples. The ground floors usually have small windows, loophole windows, and accessible only from the main door. The upper floors, on the other hand, have a geometric arrangement with many windows. Especially when a house has eight windows, then it is a multi-roomed house with a wide façade. Each room has minimum two windows.

The houses, which have two rooms on the ground floor, have a wooden staircase right opposite the main door, leading upstairs. These houses with a sofa also have two rooms upstairs. The sofa upstairs sometimes protrudes out or sometimes opens outside through a window. The windows upstairs reflect the inner arrangement because houses with no sofa-protrusion have five windows while houses with a sofa-protrusion have six windows.

Houses with three windows on their façades have a single room downstairs and a wide space for staircase leading up as well as three interconnected rooms upstairs. Another house sub-type of this type has four windows on the façade and two large and one small room upstairs.

Two houses can be considered odd and both are side by side. One is known as the 'physician's house' (no. 135, İstihlas quarter): this house stands out with its exterior decoration and triangular eaves. The second one is the so-called 'hospital' standing opposite (no. 102, İstiklal quarter) and it is closer to the houses of Izmir. Not only its details such as garden fence and consoles were manufactured in Izmir but also its type is closer to the houses of Izmir.

Some houses have curious details. House no. 94 in İstiklal quarter, within the house group above the Upper Church can be passed through underneath; hence, the passage is named 'Köprüaltı', literally "under the bridge". Just like house no. 101 in İstihlas quarter. The house is continuous upstairs but at the ground level is a street passing through it. House no. 101 also bears its date.

To the right of its doorway is engraved 1890 with trowel's point. This is an important house whose date we know.

At the corner of house no. 94 in İstiklal quarter are Byzantine architectural elements. Similarly, house no. 157 in İstiklal quarter as well as the east and west walls of the Lower Church bear Byzantine

Houses dated 1870, İstihlas Quarter.

constructional elements embedded. This understanding of conservation can be observed both at Şirince and at Selçuk.

Dido's novel mentions this tradition as follows:

"Near the village were the ruins of ancient Ephesus. To tell the truth, it did not concern us. Our village houses were already loaded with ancient decorations from their mouldings down to their thresholds..."

West, above the Upper Church, over the door of the house no. 139 is a lion figure of plaster. The wreath held by the lion is well-preserved; however, the head of the lion was broken with the greed of finding gold in it. On the eaves of this house are an indigo-blue eagle and vine rising from a vase worth noting.

Quite often in the corners are dragons made with local type tiles. Roof tiles with broken corners were placed on top of each other and with some smaller fragments placed within them they look like dragon mouths directed upward and with tongues sticking out. It was probably believed that the houses were thus protected.

Eagles seen on the eaves of some houses are also seen on the houses of Kuşadası. We have to note that these are double-headed eagles, customary since the Byzantine period.

All the door-arms, hinges etc of the doors and windows are all locally manufactured forged iron. Also yellow doorknobs and door handles, manufactured in Izmir, are seen here and there. Most of the houses are whitewashed; some are painted indigo while the so-called hospital is yellow ochre...

The school building is monumental with a fountain in the front. It stands on the ridge extending north. Its corner stones were brought over from Ayvalık's Sarımsak area. The building id flanked with terraces on the west and east. According to one information, it was built with the permission granted by Sultan Abdülaziz (1861-76). Its interior details, doors and windows make it lightful. It was taken under restoration in 1996 with the aim of establishing a local museum. However, today it serves as a restaurant.

The oil presses are single-storeyed buildings with large courts. Those still in use today have basins for salting and soaking olives in their courtyards while presses are indoors, just like regular modern oil press facilities...

CHURCHES

THE UPPER CHURCH /
CHURCH OF SAINT JOHN THE BAPTIST

Located within a courtyard the church seems to have retained almost all of its details. The school in the courtyard is used as a house today. Its door leads into a spacious living room flanked with a room on either side. Its windows facing east are located on the terrace wall where the church is located.

At the back are a terrace and a shop. The church is bounded with a terrace on the east while its west wall creates sort of a terrace between it and the houses. Access to the church is via a lean-to-roofed doorway arranged with benches. The foundation inscription is found over the arched doorway. The inscription on a marble plaque is embedded within a blind arch.

"The Church of St John the Baptist and the Prophet was built on the order of the holy priest of Heliopolis and beneficence of Kallinikos of Siphnos for the beloved Lord. It was completed with the help of precious contributions by all the Christians here and around. The church fell down after it was completed; then, a new church was built with great expenses and efforts as well as with the help of the God in the month of September in 1805."

As inferred from this inscription this church was built in September 1805 with the support of Kallinikos of Siphnos, the bishop of Heliopolis (modern Aydın). It was built in place of a former church at the same spot. Looking at the dates of earthquakes in the region, Izmir suffered from a severe earthquake on June 16th, 1778 according to the historian Slaars of Izmir. All the mosque minarets had fallen down. The earthquake repeated on the 2nd and 4th of July. All we know about the earthquakes of 1801 is that they were severe.

The date on the arch voussoirs of the gate should indicate the date of a repair or the gate itself: 1832.

The wooden lean-to roof hides an important detail: a marble head of a man embedded in the wall above the doorway. Brought from the ruins of Ephesus, the figure has a beard and recalls the ancient philosophers or even Jesus Christ depictions. As it attracted the attention of thieves, it was taken to the museum in Selçuk.

The lean-to roof is supported by cast iron water conduits, possibly from the period of the Republic. Decorated capitals are used as bases under these conduits. Perhaps this lean-to structure was originally arched, at least wooden beamed. The starting points of arches are not seen in the walls but the presence of capitals suggests a columned structure.

The prayer hall is a basilica whose three aisles are divided by two rows of 3 columns and 2 piers in each. It is covered with domes and vaults: the nave, that is the central aisle, is covered with a, from the

Upper Church, south façade.

Upper Church, main entrance.

east to the west, barrel vault, a large oval dome, two domes and a barrel vault. The north and south side aisles, on the other hand, follow a common pattern and are covered with, from the east to the west, barrel vault, a coved vault, one dome, and then barrel vault is different directions. The bench and masonry piers on the west support the wooden women's gallery. Similar masonry piers are also found on the east before the apse. Possibly the columns and piers were plastered over.

Before the restoration of the domes, pots embedded to improve the acoustics are found in them. Columns and capitals were obtained from the ruins of Ephesus including pieces from the Aydın Emirate period. On the eastern ends of the north and south walls are niches, the easternmost ones of which were indeed fountains as inferred from the holes. Water was conveyed from outside, possibly from the fountain under the plane tree on the ridge to the west. The water was conveyed through the long walls to the apse, behind the *iconostasis*. The small niches over the gate with inscription were left for checking the water flow. The apse is flanked with three niches on either side

Construction inscription dated 1805.

Repair date on the main entrance.

Cross on the keystone of the main entrance.

57

Remains of painting on the south wall.

and the central niches are larger than the other two. The small niches on the north (left) side bear frescoes of Christ while only the left small niche on the south (right) side has one.

The depiction of bearded Christ within a goblet is flanked with IΣ (Jesus) XΣ (Christ) abbreviations for his name. His halo bears the letters O, Ω, N. On the left, the frescoes bear an inscription reading "supplication of the slave of the God, the Holy Assumption." The frescoes on the south wall were about the miracles of Christ but they are poorly preserved. The dome bears traces of decoration in it centre indicating a later repair.

The apse overlooks the village through a window. The apse is flanked with colonnettes. In the middle is a Roman table foot used as the foot of the altar. The floor is paved with marble slabs or pebble mosaics. The pavement before the apse bears the holes for fitting the *iconostasis*. On the middle of the apse arch is a plaster fish figure representing the Last Supper of Christ. The women's gallery can be accessed via the staircase outside or the one inside. The wooden

Upper Church, interior.

gallery indicates the segregation between men and women during religious services in the Greek Orthodox world.

Mere coincidence, the belfry was also completed in a September. Built of marble, the belfry is composed for four posts connected with arches. Completed on the 1st of September 1876, it was commissioned by Emmanuel Marmari. Its inscription is on a marble plaque on the side of the belfry facing the courtyard. The inscription has a cross motif right in the middle. It bears signs of inexperience in the spelling of September and it is not very easy to notice the inscription at first sight. The master carved the month of September, *Septembrios* in Greek, wrong in abbreviation as "sempt". Day of the month is given as 1 with alpha, the first letter of the Greek alphabet while the year is given with Arabic numerals...

There are two decorated and inscribed pieces kept inside; one is a tombstone belonging to someone whose surname ended "...kenji". As known, Turkish was commonly spoken among the Rums of Çirkince. It is very common to come across with surnames such as *demirci* (blacksmith) or *dikenci* (thistle-trader). The second inscription bears the term *evergetai* in Greek meaning "benefactors" but where it came from is not known at all... One tombstone is embedded in the threshold of a house and it is inscribed with the name of Panagiotis G. Karakaya and the date of 1901. In the bottom line the date of ΓΔΣ 1901 inscribed with Greek letters should have been added later. The church was taken under restoration by Efes Museum in Selçuk with the support of Quatman Foundation (USA) but not completed yet.

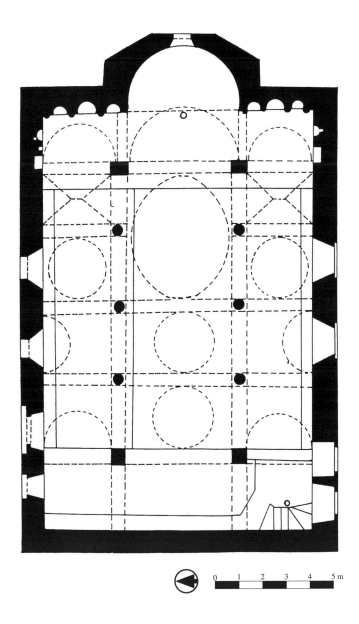

0 1 2 3 4 5 m

Plan of the Upper Church (Özgür Erol, 2000).

ST JOHN THE BAPTIST

Saint John the Baptist after whom the Upper Church of Şirince is named is not the same person as Saint John at Selçuk/Ayasuluk. St John of Ayasuluk is buried there and a church was built on his tomb and this is the Apostle John, the evangelist, the founder of the seven churches in Asia Minor. Apostle John brought Virgin Mary to Ephesus and was with her when she died. The Prophet John the Baptist is the last one to spread Judaism and to announce the coming of Christ. As mentioned in the inscription of the church, his title is *prodromos* in Greek meaning "forerunner, precursor, and harbinger". He is also known as "The Baptist" as he baptised the Israelites in the River Jordan to prepare them for the afterlife and called them to Torah as well. John was the son of Prophet Zechariah and Elizabeth, the aunt of Virgin Mary. When the Virgin visited her aunt, he saluted the Christ in his mother's womb and gave the good news. Although he is not mentioned in the Holy Qur'an, he is noted as a prophet to transmit indirectly the words of the God.

John spent his childhood and youth in the desert and started prophecy in the lower part of the Jordan Valley in 28/29 AD. Like other prophets, he wore clothes of camel hair. According to the Bible, he is "the last and the greatest prophet sent for the Kingdom of the God". After he baptised Christ, he was imprisoned by King Herod Antipas of Galilee and Jordan. When King Herod married the widow of his step-brother after the death of his own wife, John criticised him for not conforming to the traditions. Thus, a social effect of Jews and semi-Arabs uniting appeared and John was arrested and imprisoned. King Herod lost his throne when he was defeated by Aretas in 35/36. John is thought to have died before Christ did. A tomb was built by his followers and traditionally he is believed to have been buried in Samaria.

Orthodox Christians respect John for he was the precursor of Christ.

THE LOWER CHURCH / CHURCH OF SAINT DEMETRIOS

The Church of St Demetrios is mostly known as the Lower Church. It served the Muslim faith for a while as a mosque but then it was used for wedding hall and fruit storeroom. It is a single hall with two sections. There was an exonarthex with benches. Some of the six columns that once supported the entrance are lying around. On the west façade, two columns are in line flanking the main doorway; other two are at the outer corners accompanied by two others on the short sides. Stairs descending north from the main entrance led to the women's gallery. The pitched roof's west gable has fallen down.

A Byzantine plaque from the Lower Church.

The church is covered with a wooden roof. The thick walls are pierced with windows widening toward the inside. The wooden ceiling was plastered over and decorated with acanthus branches and dragons in plaster relief. The long sides have three windows reaching the iconostasis behind which is one more window on either side, summing up to eight in total on the north and south sides.

The iconostasis is carried with 12 wooden posts. The angel depictions are well-preserved under the concealing coat of paint. The iconostasis is a screen with many sacred icons and women were not allowed to go behind it. The priests conducted the mass from there, prepared

The Lower Church as in 2007.

East façade of the Lower Church.

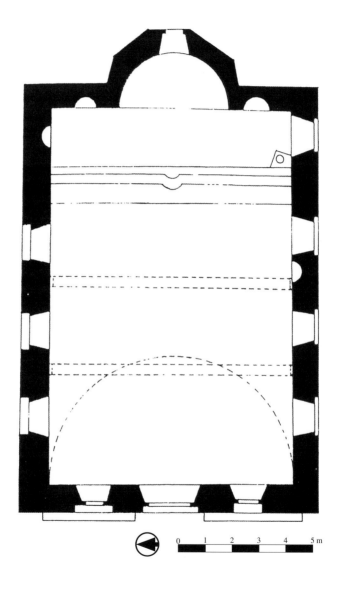

Plan of the Lower Church (Özgür Erol, 2000).

the wine and the bread for the Eucharist there. Incense and candlesticks are also kept behind there. During the mass, the clergy carried the liturgical items from there and the mass was celebrated.

The oval wooden plaques with plaster on them, 12 in total, over and between the windows once bore the depictions of the 12 apostles. On the north, depictions and names of Andrew over the second window and of Mark over the third window have survived. On the south, the name and picture of John, the old apostle, are found over the third window. The semi-circular apse on the east probably has a well before it. The window of the apse has iron lattice. Outside, on the southeast, the doorway for service and the platform that served as a minaret can be seen.

On the floor of the church, before the apse is a stone slab, a unique piece from the Aydın Emirate period. The floor is paved with stone slabs. The wooden door wings decorated with the meander motifs were stolen about 1992. Perhaps they are kept in a private collection in Turkey. Perhaps they will emerge one day again. The building is left to its fate and the roof does not give the feeling that it will survive for long. The villagers sell their handicrafts in front of the church...

DEPARTURE

Western Turkey was occupied by the Greeks on the 15th of May, 1915 and this invasion came to an end on the 9th of September, 1922 when Turkish army took over Izmir. The news of Turkish takeover reached Athens on the 11th via a news from Paris. Greek newspaper Elephtero Bima passed the Paris origin news of 10th September as "Izmir has come under the occupation of Zeki Bey, the commander of the 2nd Cavalcade, as of yesterday morning. Everything is under the control of the Turkish army."

The pull-out of the Greek army had started earlier than the capture of Izmir; but the massacres and destruction they caused while withdrawing caused the local Rums abandon their homes too. As the Greek army withdrew, the local Rums grew more worried and used whatever vehicles they could find – horse carriages, train – but mainly on foot, left their homes with whatever they could take with them. Izmir suddenly became the scene of a tumult. Following the 9th of September, many left by sea, with whatever boat or ship they could get hold of. Those who left Turkey from Çeşme and Ayvalık, first reached the islands, and then to Piraeus harbour. The great fire of Izmir that broke out on the 13th of September was another catastrophe adding up to all that was going on.

As Dido Sotiriou wrote at the end of her novel, the fire started in Hagios Dimitrios quarter, that is, the Armenian quarter of Izmir. It was initiated by Armenian terrorists. It spread quickly thanks to an unusual wind from the southeast. Starting around the main train station at Basmahane it quickly reached the Promenade via the Fevzi Paşa Boulevard, and north, to Bella Vista (modern Gündoğdu) via the fairground.

This is known as the Catastrophe of Asia Minor. The people of Çirkince probably arrived in Izmir by train during this catastrophe. Here are some details not to our liking. Manoli Axiotis, our hero of the novel, passed to Samos Island via Güzelçamlı south of Kuşadası and reached Greece. On the way of flight with a friend, he thought of stopping at the village:

"Near Kirkija, our hearts pounded a bit. When we understood there was nobody in the village, we wandered around for a while. Indeed, we were like two thieves under the walls. The moon was shining and we were able to see the wooden door wings creaking with the wind. It was as if there were a plague prevailing in the village and all living beings had been taken away! In the market area, in the main square, in the streets were lots of unowned garments, house wares, broken pots. A dog barked now and then, a cat meowed, and the loneliness became unbearable... Here, every house, every street, every tree, every stone of this earth was beaten with our hearts, with our memories...

"Anger grew suddenly in us: were these houses not ours? These fields, these crops, this tree? Have we not grown up here? Have we not spent our efforts here? Were our fathers not buried here?"

Here, whether from the real memories of Manoli or from her own, Sotiriou wrote about the pain of leaving behind. Unfortunately, Turks who had to leave their home similarly would come to the same village a year later.

Visit cars of Hadji Demetrios, headman of the Hagios Demetrios Quarter where the Izmir fire of 1922 started.

POPULATION EXCHANGE BETWEEN GREECE AND TURKEY

"Convention and Protocol Concerning the Exchange of Greek and Turkish Populations", an appendix to the Treaty of Lausanne, was undersigned on January 30th 1923. It was undersigned by M. İsmet, Dr. Rıza Nur and Hasan on behalf of the National Assembly of Turkey, and by Venizelos and Kaklamanos on behalf of Greece. Turkish nationals of Greek Orthodox religion settled in Istanbul and Greek nationals of Moslem religion settled in western Thrace were exempted. Those who left their homes as of 1912 were included within this treaty and considered refugees. Those who were given priority to leave Turkey were those whose families had already gone to Greece. Around September 9th, 1922, the Rums of Turkey, above all those in west Anatolia, had already abandoned their homes and fields thanks to the defeat of the Greek army. The Rums living in Muğla, Konya and Antalya abided by the deportation enforced by the Treaty of Lausanne. The convention protected all judicial rights of both the Rums and Turks. The rights and trials of those who were being tried at the court were transferred to their new home country. Portable goods of the refugees were exempted from customs tax. Both sides were allowed to take the official belongings of churches, mosques and associations. Their real estates were recorded by committees and were replaced by similar property in the new country. Committees prepared certificates valuing such properties. The convention stated that in case necessary, money would be paid for the property left behind.

On October 13th, 1923, the Ministry of Exchange Zoning and Settlement and the Act of Exchange Zoning and Settlement passed on November 8th, 1923. The minister was Mustafa Necati, deputy from Izmir, asked for assistance of the Turkish Red Crescent and the protocol for cooperation between the Ministry and the Red Crescent was undersigned on March 6th, 1924. Izmir was the settlement region no. 4 and İhsan Pasha was appointed as its director, who arrived in the region and started working right away on November 26th, 1923. The abandoned buildings on the Promenade were given to the order of the Ministry;

the contagious diseases hospital at Tepecik, Izmir, was prepared for the newcomers; the guesthouse at Klazumen (modern Urla) was prepared and necessary measures were taken. The hospitals at Torbalı and Tepeköy were prepared for malaria. Tea, soup, clothes etc to be distributed to the newcomers were procured together with the Red Crescent. Temporary shelters were constructed at Çeşme and Bayındır with the metal sheets procured from the British. The dispensary at İkiçeşmelik and the one established at Kemer Station started serving the newcomers' health problems toward the end of December 1923.

The exchange was decided to start on November 10th, 1923. On the Greek side, temporary shelters were established for 1500 people at Kozana, 1000 people at Karaferye station and 1000 people at Ahdova. Necessary tents and other materials were distributed to the departure ports and stations. By the end of 1923, 60,318 refugees were brought to Turkey with Turkish ships and trains from Crete, Kavala, Drama and Thessaloniki. Despite the severe winter of 1923-24, the transportations continued non-stop. Moving was completed toward the end of 1924.

However, things did not develop as comfortable as thought. There was turmoil in some parties. People from the same village had to embark on different ships. Claims of some who owned nothing were taken into consideration and they were given property. Most of the newcomers were workers; only very few were involved in commerce;

Teacher, students and the Şirince people welcoming the governor Kazım Dirik (about 1930)

some were in need of help. Some arrived in Turkey with all their belongings gone. Preparations on both sides were underqualified. Tobacco workers were settled up the mountains. The refugees set foot on major ports such as Ayvalık, Erdek, Çeşme and Izmir in very poor condition. The aid by the Red Crescent continued until 1933.

As a result, 500,000 people were brought to Turkey from Greece by ships or trains. Within this turmoil, refugees from Thessaloniki, Monastir and Provushta came to Şirince. According to what is told, villagers from Kavala, Kula, Dedebal, Alasonya, Drama, Mushtiyan,

Turkish refugees, students and the Governor Kazım Dirik in front of the Şirince Pirmary School (about 1930).

Doryan and Çıtak boarded on the same ship and arrived in Izmir. Half of Mushtiyan were Rums while other villages were small size villages of about 30 households. All the immigrants boarded on the Akdeniz and reached Izmir. After staying at Kemer for a while, they were allowed to go wherever they liked. While some settled in Ödemiş some came from Atça, Aydın, and settled at Çirkince. The notables of the immigrants came to the village with no road but when they saw that it was a well-built village, they settled. Those from Crete came to Kuşadası sailing on a ship together with animals and goods.

KAZIM PASHA NAMES THE VILLAGE

Time for a change in name. Kazım Pasha, the governor of Izmir, was born in Monastir in 1879. He graduated from the military college in 1899 as infantry lieutenant. He fought at the Balkan Wars and then at Gallipoli. He disembarked at Samsun together with Mustafa Kemal on the 19th of May, 1919. During the National Independence War, he served as the commander of army transport corps in west Anatolia. He was appointed to Izmir on March 27th, 1926 and served there as the governor until August 7th, 1935. His extraordinary efforts of service include the constructions of about 200 schools, numerous streets and fountains.

The story goes that Governor Kazım Dirik changed the name of Çirkince to Şirince. He commented that such a beautiful place must not be called ugly, can only be called lovely. He was inspired by the march written by Suat Bey, the teacher of the primary school. The march called the village "şirince" meaning lovely. This name change is described in the story by Sabahattin Ali as the politicians visiting the village and changing its name.

Governor Kazım Dirik together with Şirince people at Ephesus (abour 1930).

The march by Suat Bey, the teacher:

Köyümüz şeref saçar (Our village honours)
Yaylaların üstüne. (the pastures)
Küme küme kuş uçar (Birds fly in groups)
Tarlaların üstüne. (over the fields)

Soğuk kaynak suları (Cold spring waters)
Şırıl şırıl şırıldar. (babble pleasantly)
Söğütlerin dalları (Willows' branches)
Sulara gölge yapar. (shade over the waters)

Kimdir diyen acaba (Who is it, really)
Bu yerlere Çirkince (who called these lands "ugly"?)
Biz diyelim daima (Let us call always)
Köyümüze Şirince (our village "lovely")

Gece gökte yıldızlar (Stars are diamonds)
Birer elmas parçası (of the skies at night)
Her tarafı yaldızlar. (glazing all over)
Hain altın fırçası. (Deceitful golden brush)

Kaval ile çobanlar (Shepherds playing their flutes)
Dağdan dağa seslenir. (call from mountain to mountain)
Sürü sürü koyunlar (Flocks of sheep)
Yamaçlarda beslenir. (graze on the slopes)

Kimdir diyen acaba (Who is it, really)
Bu yerlere Çirkince, (who called these lands "ugly"?)
Biz diyelim daima (Let us call always)
Köyümüze Şirince (our village "lovely")

SABAHATTİN ALİ
1907-1945

Sabahattin Ali is the only Turkish author who wrote about Şirince in early "post-Rum" times. He was born in Gümülcine (modern Komotini in Greece) on February 25th, 1907. He graduated from teachers' school at Istanbul in 1927 and went to Germany on passing the exams of the Ministry of Education. When he was teaching at a secondary school in Aydın, he was imprisoned for three months because of one of his writings. After 1933, he worked at the Ministry of Education, Directorate of School Books and Directorate of Publications. He taught German at Ankara, worked as a translator and as a play writer at Ankara State Conservatory. His first poem was published in *Çağlayan* magazine in Balıkesir. He was killed in 1948.

His novels: *Kuyucaklı Yusuf* (*Yusuf of Kuyucak*, 1937), *İçimizdeki Şeytan* (*The Devil inside Us*, 1940), *Kürk Mantolu Madonna* (*Madonna with Fur Coat*, 1943).

His story books: *Değirmen* (*Mill*, 1935), *Kağnı* (*Oxcart*, 1936), *Ses* (*Voice*, 1937), *Yeni Dünya* (*The New World*, 1943), *Sırça Köşk* (*Crystal Mansion*, 1980).

His poems are collected in *Dağlar ve Rüzgâr* (*Mountains and the Wind*), *Kurbağanın Serenadı* (*Serenade of the Frog*), *Öteki Şiirler* (*Other Poems*, 1980). He also wrote a play *Esirler* (*Slaves*, 1966).

ŞİRİNCE, THE VILLAGE OF THE IMMIGRANTS

One of Sabahattin Ali's stories in *Crystal Mansion* is called *Çirkince* after the village. Details of Şirince's past after the Rums emerge in this story very curiously. When Sabahattin Ali was 9, his father, who was an officer in the Ottoman army, sent him, the mother and the 5-year-old brother to Çivril from Çanakkale. From Çanakkale they went to Bandırma on a gunboat and then took the train to Izmir. Then they got on the Aydın train to go to Çivril, to their grandfather but the locomotive broke down so they had to stay there for a few days until the train was repaired. As the repair took long, a captain serving there took them to Çirkince as guests to his own home. They spent some time together with the officer's family there and continued their train journey.

About 30 years later, Sabahattin Ali went to Şirince to spend some time until the departure of the train to Ankara. The train would start off about midnight from Izmir and reach Ayasuluk a few hours later. Thus, Sabahattin Ali thought that he could catch the train at Ayasuluk. So he came early in the morning and first visited the ruins of Ephesus, then could not resist and went to Şirince. There he found the oldest immigrant of the village, the Cretan who was running the coffee house and chatted with him…

"This was not the place I had seen thirty years earlier, where I had spent the most beautiful days of my life. Those four walls on the right, rising without its doors, windows and roof, could not be the school where the children played. At the foot of the grant plane tree before me was a marble fountain with four taps, not a heap of stones in a marsh.

"Now lived maybe only 50 families here, in this small town of 800 houses. The refugees settled here sold their fig orchards and olive groves for almost nothing for they knew only how to grow the tobacco, even cut most of the trees in the winter and burnt them, then each one went somewhere else…"

Sabahattin Ali observed through this and other details both the wounds opened with the exchange and how Şirince deteriorated afterwards.

Sabahattin Ali continued his chat with the Cretan man running the coffee house which does not exist any more…

"The refugees settled here were not guilty either. They were tobacco farmers from İskeçe (modern Xanthi in Greece) and Kavala… They did not understand how to deal with olives and figs… Trees demand care, demand spending… Trees do not provide those who do not know their value… When the refugees did not receive produce for two years, they either cut down the trees or sold them… When ignorance joined poverty, the wealth of Sultan Süleyman the Magnificent dissolved…"

Şirince really dissolved and deteriorated. Some pulled down their houses for its wood and tiles and abandoned while some others did not pay any attention at all. Consequently, what remains today has survived thanks to the personal efforts and resistance of Şirince people. Thus, we learn two pitiful stories, what was experienced at Şirince by two different societies, from two different authors…

RECOMMENDED TOURING

We recommend that the travellers visiting Şirince should start from the courtyard of the former primary school, now a restaurant. It is a real delight to watch the village and the surrounding landscape from here. Then continue up to the Lower Church. From the outer benches of the church you can view the environs. Women of Şirince sell their handcrafts, home made wine, olives and olive oil here. When you continue further up, then you will first reach a home renowned for hospitality. This is where the Turkish movie *Başka Olur Ağaların Düğünü* was shot. Curious to watch its carved window shutters... Opposite it is the so-called hospital, now restored.

The Upper Church has been restored to some extent and although it could not become a museum, it still has a special place. It has water in its courtyard and shopping is also possible here. It is worthwhile to go to the street up from the church and have a look at the houses there. Here you will find decorated Byzantine stones, lion relief, birds on the eaves and the passageway under the house... It is possible to dine around here too. Home made ham beans in olive oil, stuffed vine leaves as fine as the small finger, *gözleme*, *ayran* and home wine should be tasted. The home wine can be easily recognised with its slightly cloudy look, sugary taste and little gaseousness.

You can reach the village square via the street below the church, behind the mosque. Or, you can continue further south and pas to the other quarter via the stream bed. Watching the twin grand house (no. 156) there, continue along the Çamaşırhane Sokak (Laundry Street). Then you will see the street passing under house no. 101 and reach the village square passing in between the restaurants.

You can also make the same tour in the reverse direction by leaving your car in the village car park and starting with the house no. 101 in İstihlas quarter.

The minibuses running between Şirince and Selçuk start off in the small square behind the mosque. In the square too you have a chance for buying the handcrafts, vines, olives, edible weeds etc. The local bakery sells delicious local bread. You can also find some figs, not as beautiful as before though. In the recent years, wine production has developed enormously. Some shops allow you to taste first.

There is no special souvenir of Şirince. We will recommend once again that you experience a nice shopping with local women and chat with them.

Increasing numbers of houses are restored day by day. However, ugly attempts also exist. Pensions for staying overnight also proliferate.

FURTHER READING

Sabahattin Türkoğlu, *Efes'in Öyküsü [The Story of Ephesus]*, Arkeoloji ve Sanat Yayınları, Istanbul 1991.

W. Alzinger, *Die Stadt Des Siebenten Weltwunders, Die Wiederentdeckung von Ephesos*, Wien 1962.

Meyers Reisebücher, Griechenland und Kleinasien bibliographische Institut, Leipzig und Wien 1904.

[Evliya Çelebi], *Evliya Çelebi Seyahatnamesi, Comparison of Manuscripts Topkapı Sarayı Kütüphanesi Bağdat 306, Süleymaniye Kütüphanesi Pertev Paşa 462, Süleymaniye Kütüphanesi Hacı Beşir Ağa 452, Their Transcription and Index*, prepared by Yücel Dağlı - Seyit Ali Kahraman - Robert Dankoff, YKY Istanbul 2005, 71-72.

Prof. Dr. Ünal Öziş, *Su Mühendisliği Açısından Anadolu'daki Eski Su Yapıları [Ancient Water Works of Anatolia from the Point of Water Engineering]*, DEÜ Mühendislik-Mimarlık Fakültesi Yayınları, No: 73, 1987 Izmir.

Dr. Erol Atalay, "Ephesos Yöresinde Antik Mağaralar [Ancient Caves around Ephesus]", *I. Araştırma Sonuçları Toplantısı*, 1983, 105.

Dr. Erol Atalay, "Sütini ve Kemalpaşa Mağaralarında Bulunan Bizans Freskleri [Byzantine Frescoes at Sütini and Kemalpaşa Caves]", *II. Araştırma Sonuçları Toplantısı*, 1984, 63.

Doç. Dr. Zeynep Mercangöz, "Efes ve Çevresinde Hristiyanlık (Ortaçağ Hristiyan dönemde Efes ve Ayasuluğ [Christianity in and around Ephesus (Ephesus and Ayasuluğ in Medieval Christian Times)], Uluslararası Birinci Geçmişten Günümüze Selçuk Sempozyumu, Izmir 1997, 51.

Georgios Nakracas, *Anadolu ve Rum Göçmenlerinin Kökeni [The Origins of the Anatolian and Rum Refugees]*, Belge Yayınları İstanbul 2003, 98.

Prof. Dr. Reinhard Stewig, *Batı Anadolu'nun Kültürel Gelişmesi: Kartoğrafik Bilgiler [Cultural Development of West Anatolia: Cartographic Information]*, transl. Ruhi Turfan, Türkiye Turing Otomobil Kurumu. [Istanbul undated]

Dr. Himmet Akın, *Aydınoğulları Tarihi Hakkında Bir Araştırma [A Study on the History of Aydın Emirate]*, 1968 Ankara.

Our Lady of Ephesus, Bernard F. Deutsch, 1965, Milwaukiee.

Fügen İlter, "Bazı Örneklerle Osmanlı Dönemi Mimarlığında XIX. Yüzyıl Ege Bölgesi Kiliseleri: Gökçeada (İmroz)- Ayvalık - Selçuk Şirince (Kırkıca) Köyü [19th Century Churches in the Aegean Region in the Light of Some Examples: Gökçeada (Imbros)- Ayvalık - Selçuk Şirince (Kırkıca)", *XI. Türk Tarih Kongresi*, Vol. V.

Sasa Tsakiri, Dido Sotiriou - Apo ton Kypo tis Edem sto Kamini tou Aiona mas [From the Garden of Eden to the Fire of the Century], Kedros, 1996 Athens.

Dido Sotiriyu, *Benden Selam Söyle Anadolu'ya [Farewell Anatolia]*, Transl: Atilla Tokatlı, Alan Yayıncılık, 8th edition, Istanbul 1992.

Sabahattin Ali, *Sırça Köşk [Crystal Mansion]*, Sabahattin Ali, Bütün Eserleri 8, Cem Yayınevi, Istanbul 1987

Filiz Ali, "Filiz Hiç Üzülmesin", *Sabahattin Ali'nin Objektifinden, Kızı Filiz'in Gözünden Bir Yaşam Öyküsü [A Life Story from the Objective of Sabahattin Ali and from the Eyes of His Daughter Filiz]*, Sel Yayıncılık, Istanbul 1995.

Edmund D. Chishull, *Türkiye Gezisi ve İngiltere'ye Dönüş [Journey to Turkey and Return to England]*, Transl: Bahattin Orhon, Istanbul 1993.

F.V.J. Arundell, *Discoveries in Asia Minor*, in two volumes, London 1834, 262-274.

Prof. Dr. A. Haluk Sezgin, *Turquie, Architecture traditionelle des Balkans*, Edition Melissa, Athenes 1992.

Kevork Pamukciyan, "İzmir'in Büyük Yer Sarsıntıları [Great Earthquakes of Izmir]", *Tarih ve Toplum*, October 1989.

İsmail Soysal, *Türkiye'nin Dış Münasebetleriyle İlgili Başlıca Siyasi Andlaşmalar [Main International Political Conventions of Turkey]*, İş Bankası Kültür Yayınları, Ankara 1965.

Kemal Arı, *Büyük Mübadele Türkiye'ye Zorunlu Göç [The Great Exchange, Forced Migration to Turkey] (1923-1925)*, Tarih Vakfı Yurt Yayınları, Istanbul 1995.

Şirince'de Tarihsel Dokunun Korunması ve Turizm Amaçlı Kullanımı [Conservation of the Historical Texture of Şirince and Its Touristic Use], Kültür ve Turizm Bakanlığı, Planlama ve Yatırımlar Dairesi Başkanlığı, Araştırma Grup Başkanlığı Yayın No: 1983/3.

Arman Özgür Erol, *Ege Bölgesi Rum Ortodoks Kiliseleri [Greek orthodox Churches in the Aegean Region]*, Ege University, Institute of Social Sciences, unpublished master's thesis, Izmir 2003.

R. Funda Barbaros, *1830-1930 Döneminde Sosyo-Ekonomik Çözüm Arayışları Çerçevesinde İzmir'de Sanayileşme [Industrialisation in Izmir within the Frame of Search for Socio-economic Solutions between 1830-1930]*, EBSO Yayını, Izmir 1995.

I Zmirni Kegete (in Greek), compiled by I. K. Mazarakis, Athens 1983.

Mehmet Ali Keskin, *İzmir Valileri [Governors of Izmir]*, Izmit 1989.

Güney Dinç, *Yedi Domuzlu Altın [Gold with Seven Pigs]*, Bilgi Yayınevi, Ankara 1989.

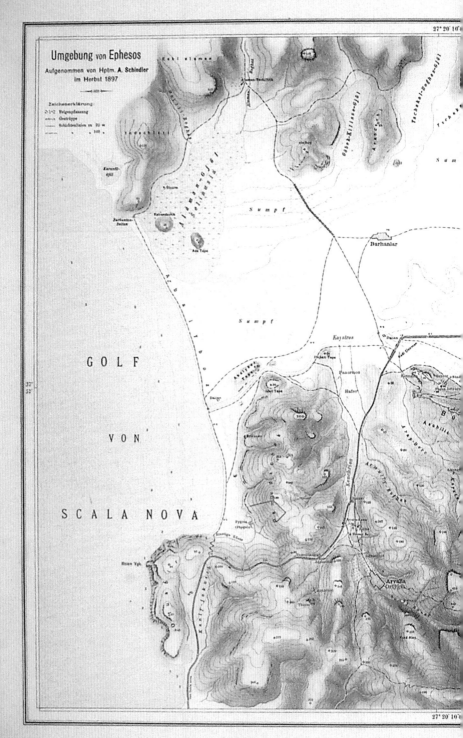

Umgebung von Ephesos

Aufgenommen von Hptm. A. Schindler
im Herbst 1897

Zeichenerklärung:

GOLF

VON

SCALA NOVA

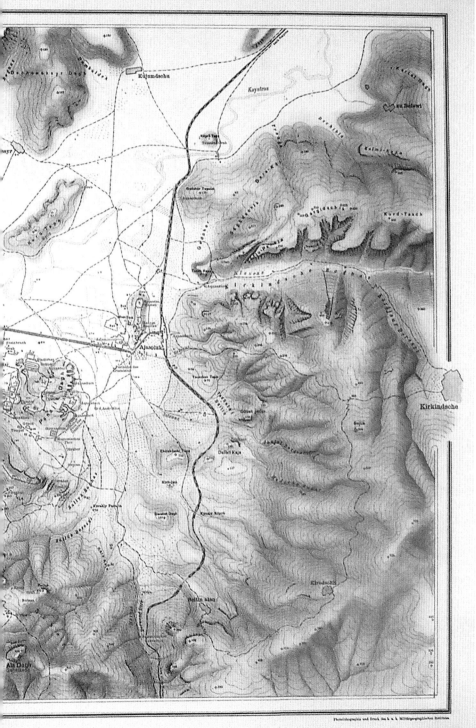

Kirkindsche

Photolithographie und Druck des k. u. k. Militärgeographischen Institutes.